D0909813

J   93-4234
553.6   Mitgutsch, Ali
MIT   From sea to Salt

Lyons, Nebr.

1. Books may be kept two weeks and may
be renewed once for the same period, except
7 day books and magazines.

2. A fine is charged for each day a book is
not returned according to the above rule. No
book will be issued to any person incurring
such a fine until it has been paid.

3. All injuries to books beyond reasonable
wear and all losses shall be made good to the
satisfaction of the Librarian.

4. Each borrower is held responsible for
all books charged on his card and for all fines
accruing on the same.

From Sea to Salt

From Sea to Salt

Ali Mitgutsch

Carolrhoda Books, Inc., Minneapolis

Little Priest
Tribal College Library
Winnebago, Nebraska

Gift

1993

First published in the United States of America 1985 by Carolrhoda Books, Inc.
Original edition © 1982 by Sellier Verlag GmbH, Eching bei München,
West Germany, under the title VOM MEER ZUM SALZ.
Revised English text © 1985 by Carolrhoda Books, Inc.
Illustrations © 1982 by Sellier Verlag GmbH.
All rights reserved.

Manufactured in the United States of America

LIBRARY OF CONGRESS CATALOGING IN PUBLICATION DATA

Mitgutsch, Ali.
  From sea to salt.

    (A Carolrhoda start to finish book)
    Rev. English text of: Vom Meer zum Salz.
    SUMMARY: Describes the methods used to extract
salt from the sea and from deep underground mines.

    1. Salt — Juvenile literature. [1. Salt]
I. Title.   II. Series.

TN900.M5813   1985   553.6′3   84-17466
ISBN 0-87614-232-3 (lib. bdg.)

  1 2 3 4 5 6 7 8 9 10 94 93 92 91 90 89 88 87 86 85

From Sea to Salt

Salt comes from the sea.

If you have ever swallowed ocean water,

then you know how salty the sea is.

In hot, sunny climates, it is easy to get salt from the sea.

Seawater is let into shallow basins through little gates.

Then the gates are closed.

The water is trapped inside.

After several hours in the sun, the water will dry up.

We say that the water has **evaporated**.

The salt does not evaporate.

It is left behind in the basins.

Salt can also be found deep under the ground.

That salt also came from the sea.

Millions of years ago,

oceans covered land that is now dry.

At that time, the surface of the earth
was always moving and shifting.
Sometimes the land rose above the sea
and trapped some seawater in lakes or ponds.
When that water evaporated, salt was left behind.
As the land kept moving, the salt was buried.

Today people mine the salt that is buried in the earth.
First a hollow room is dug under the ground
where the salt is.
Then two pipes are run down into the room.
Water is pumped into the room through one pipe.
The salt dissolves in the water
just as sugar dissolves in coffee.
This salty water is called **brine**.
The brine is pumped out of the ground
through the second pipe.

The salt and water must now be separated again.
To do this, the brine is boiled in a large container
until the water evaporates.
The salt is left behind.

Before it can be packaged, the salt must be cleaned.

Then the coarse salt grains must be ground up.

Finally the salt is put into packages

and delivered to stores where we can buy it.

Salt is used for many things.
Chemicals that come from salt
are used to make paper, plastics, soap, and glass.
Coarse, unclean salt is used to melt ice off roads.
And, of course, we put salt in our food
to make it taste better.
The next time you sprinkle salt on your French fries,
take a moment to think about where it came from.

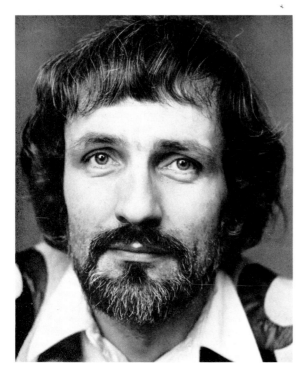

Ali
Mitgutsch

ALI MITGUTSCH is one of Germany's best-known
children's book illustrators. He is a devoted world traveler, and
many of his book ideas have taken shape during his travels.
Perhaps this is why they have such international appeal.
Mr. Mitgutsch's books have been published in 22 countries
and are enjoyed by thousands of readers around the world.

Ali Mitgutsch lives with his wife and three children in
Schwabing, the artists' quarter in Munich. The Mitgutsch
family also enjoys spending time on their farm in the Bavarian
countryside.

THE CAROLRHODA

>>> START

TO FINISH >>>

BOOKS